Guitar • Vocal

STRUM & SING

The Who

Lyrics, Chord Symbols and
Guitar Chord Diagrams for 20 Hit Songs

T0087361

Cover photo:Tom Hill/WireImage

ISBN 978-1-60378-994-3

HAL•LEONARD®

Visit Hal Leonard Online at
www.halleonard.com

Contact Us:
Hal Leonard
7777 West Bluemound Road
Milwaukee, WI 53213
Email: info@halleonard.com

In Europe contact:
Hal Leonard Europe Limited
42 Wigmore Street
Marylebone, London, W1U 2RN
Email: info@halleonardeurope.com

In Australia contact:
Hal Leonard Australia Pty. Ltd.
4 Lentara Court
Cheltenham, Victoria, 3192 Australia
Email: info@halleonard.com.au

Contents

Baba O'Riley

Words and Music by
Peter Townshend

(Capo 1st fret)

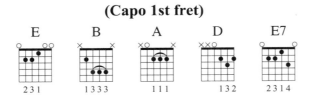

| E | B | A | D | E7 |

Intro   ‖:E   B |A |E   B |A   :‖ *Play 4 times*

Verse 1

E   B |A |E
　　Out here in the fields
　　　　B |A |E
I fight for my meals.
　　　　B |A
I get my ___ back
　　|E   B |A |E
Into my living.
　　　　B |A |E
I don't need to fight
　　　　B |A |E
To prove ___ I'm right.
　　　　B |A
I don't ___ need
　　|E   B |A   ‖
To be for - given.

Interlude 1   ‖:E   B |A   :‖ *Play 5 times*

‖:B | :‖

Bridge

N.C. | | |
Don't cry; ___ don't raise your eye.
　| | | | ‖
It's only teenage wasteland.

Verse 2

  E   B |A |E
   Sally, take my hand,

        B |A |
We'll travel south, 'cross land.

  E   B
Put out the fire

  |A |E B|A |E
And don't look past my shoul - der.

      B |A |E
The exodus is here;

      B |A |
The happy ones are near.

  E   B
Let's get together

  |A |E B|A   ‖
Be - fore we get much old - er.

Guitar Solo

|E B |A B |E B |A

Chorus

      ‖E B |A
Teenage wasteland;

      B |E B |A
It's only teen - age wasteland.

    B |E B |A
Teen - age wasteland;

    B |E B|A
Teen - age wasteland.

    B ‖
They're all…

Interlude 2

|B |A |
 Wasted!

‖:B |A |E |D   :‖

Violin Solo

|E | |D | |

‖:N.C.(E) | | :‖ *Play 3 times*

‖:E7 | | | :‖

|B | | |E N.C. ‖

Bargain

Words and Music by
Peter Townshend

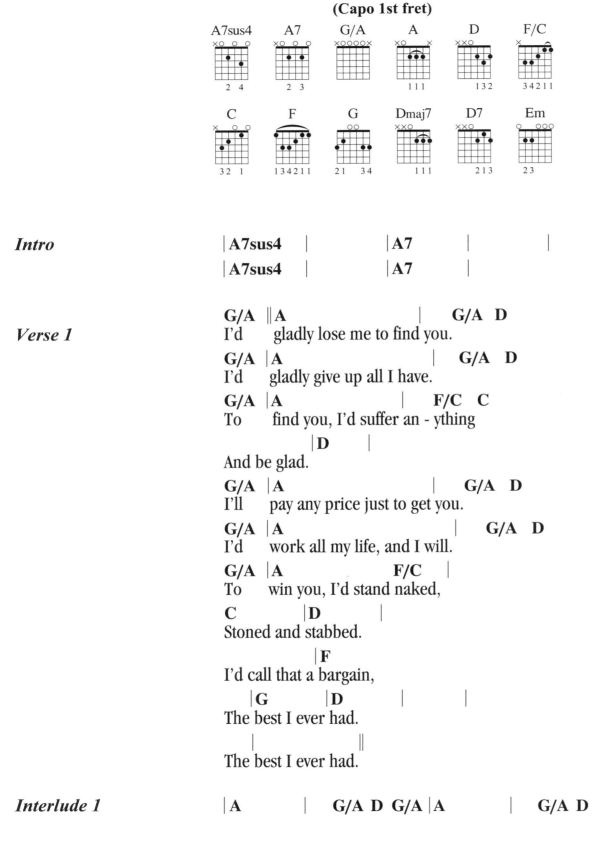

(Capo 1st fret)

A7sus4   A7   G/A   A   D   F/C

C   F   G   Dmaj7   D7   Em

Intro

|A7sus4 | |A7 | | |
|A7sus4 | |A7 | |

Verse 1

G/A ‖A | G/A D
I'd   gladly lose me to find you.

G/A |A | G/A D
I'd   gladly give up all I have.

G/A |A | F/C C
To   find you, I'd suffer an - ything

            |D |
And be glad.

G/A |A | G/A D
I'll   pay any price just to get you.

G/A |A | G/A D
I'd   work all my life, and I will.

G/A |A   F/C |
To   win you, I'd stand naked,

C |D |
Stoned and stabbed.

        |F
I'd call that a bargain,

    |G |D | |
The best I ever had.

        | ‖
The best I ever had.

Interlude 1

|A | G/A D G/A |A | G/A D

Verse 2

```
G/A ‖A                    |          G/A   D
I'd    gladly lose me to find you,
G/A |A                    |          G/A   D
'N'    gladly give up all I got.
G/A |A                         |F/C
To    catch you, I'm gonna run
      C      |D              |
'N' never stop.
G/A |A                         |          G/A   D
I'll    pay any price just to win you,
G/A |A                    |          G/A   D
Sur  -  render my good life for bad.
G/A |A                    |F/C
To    find you, I'm gonna drown
      C      |D              |
An unsung man.
                    |F
I call that a bargain,
   |G           |D          |          |
The best I ever had.
      |              ‖
The best I ever had.
```

Guitar Solo 1

```
|A              |     G/A  D  G/A |A              |     G/A  D  ‖
```

Bridge

```
D                        |Dmaj7
   I sit lookin' 'round,
                              |D7                 |
I look at my face ___ in the mirror.
                         |G      |     |C         |
I know I'm worth nothing with - out you.
                   |D                         |Dmaj7
And like      one and one don't make two,
                         |D7           |
One and one make one.
      |G           |          |C        |
And I'm lookin' for that free ___ ride to me,
                         |Em      |          ‖
I'm lookin' for you.
```

Interlude 2

```
‖: A              |          |A7sus4      |
   |              |A7        |          ‖
```

Synth Solo 1	‖: A7sus4 |	|A7 |	:‖ *Play 3 times*
	| A7sus4 |	|A7 |	

Verse 3

               G/A ‖A   \| G/A   D   G/A \|
I'd   gladly lose me to find you.

A   \| G/A   D
Gladly give up all I got.

G/A \|A   \|F/C
To   catch you, I'm gonna run

             C   \|D   \|
And ___ never stop.

    \|A   \| G/A   D
I'll pay any price just I to win you,

G/A \|A   \| G/A   D
Sur - render my good life for bad.

G/A \|A   \|F/C
To   find you, I'm gonna drown

             C   \|D   \|
An unsung man.

                     \|F
I'd call that a bargain,

    \|G   \|D   \| \| \|
The best I ever had.

    \| \| \| \|

        \| ‖
The best I ever had.

Guitar Solo 2	|A | G/A D G/A |A	| G/A D G/A |	
	|A | G/A D G/A |A	| G/A D ‖	
Interlude 3	‖: A7sus4 |	|A7 |	:‖
Synth Solo 2	‖: A7sus4 |	|A7 |	:‖ *Play 4 times*
Guitar Solo 3	‖: A7sus4 |	|A7 |	:‖ *Play 3 times*
	|A7sus4 |	‖	
Outro	|A |A7sus4	|A7 |	|
	|A7sus4 |	|A7 |	|
	|A7sus4 |	|A7 ‖	

Eminence Front

Words and Music by
Peter Townshend

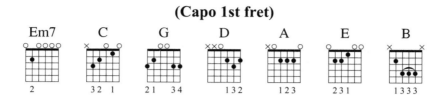

(Capo 1st fret)

Em7   C   G   D   A   E   B

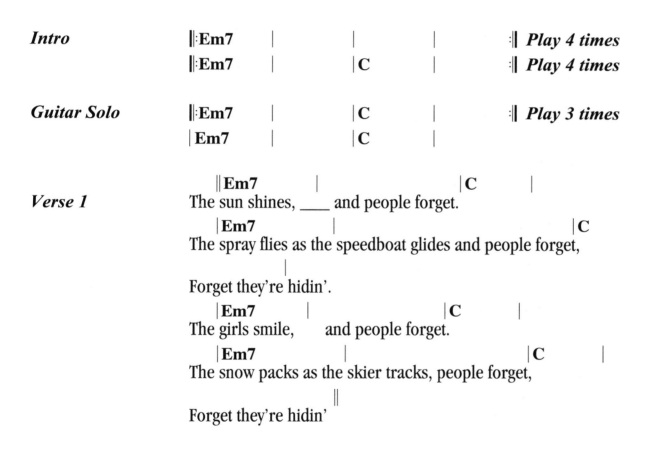

Intro

‖: Em7 | | | :‖ *Play 4 times*
‖: Em7 | |C | :‖ *Play 4 times*

Guitar Solo

‖: Em7 | |C | :‖ *Play 3 times*
|Em7 | |C |

Verse 1

‖ Em7 | |C |
The sun shines, ___ and people forget.

|Em7 | |C
The spray flies as the speedboat glides and people forget,

|
Forget they're hidin'.

|Em7 | |C |
The girls smile,   and people forget.

|Em7 | |C |
The snow packs as the skier tracks, people forget,

‖
Forget they're hidin'

Chorus 1

Em7 |
Behind an eminence front.   Eminence front,
        |C | |Em7
It's a put on.

                |
It's an eminence front,   It's an eminence front,
        |C | |Em7
It's a put on.

                |
An eminence front,   eminence front,
        |C | |Em7
It's a put on, ____ eminence front.

                |
It's an eminence front,   it's an eminence front,
        |C | ‖
It's a put on. ____ It's a put on.   It's a put on. It's a put on.

Interlude |G D A G |D A E   ‖

Bridge 1

Em7 |
Come and join the party
       |C |
Dressed to kill.
      |Em7 |
Won't you come and join the party
       |C | |B | | | ‖
Dressed to kill?   Dressed to kill.

Verse 2

Em7 | |C |
Drinks flow,   people forget.
   |Em7 | |C
That big wheel spins,   the hair thins, and people forget
        |
Forget they're hidin'.
   |Em7 | |C |
The news slows,   people forget.
   |Em7 | |C
The shares crash, hopes are dashed, people for - get.
        | ‖
Forget they're hidin'

Chorus 2

Em7 |
    Behind an eminence front.   An eminence front,
        |**C** | |**Em7**
It's a put on.

                                    |
It's an eminence front,   Eminence front,
        |**C** | |**Em7**
It's a put on.

                                    |
An eminence front,   An eminence front,
        |**C** | |**Em7**
It's a put on.

                            |
Eminence front,   it's an eminence front,
        |**C** | ‖
It's a put on.   It's a put on. It's a put on.   It's a put on.

Bridge 2

Em7 | |
Come and join the party dressed to,
C | |
Come and join the party dressed to,
Em7 | |
Come on, join the party dressed to,
C |
Come and join the party
                |**B** | |
Dressed to kill.
                        | |**Em7** N.C. ‖
Dress yourself to kill.

Behind Blue Eyes

Words and Music by
Peter Townshend

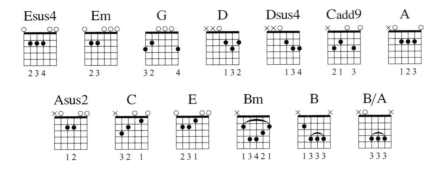

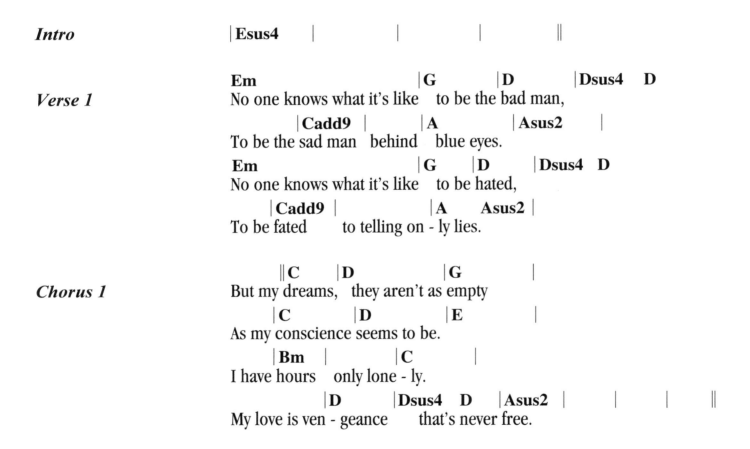

Intro |Esus4 | | | ||

Verse 1

Em |G |D |Dsus4   D
No one knows what it's like   to be the bad man,
          |Cadd9 | |A |Asus2 |
To be the sad man   behind   blue eyes.
Em |G |D |Dsus4   D
No one knows what it's like   to be hated,
          |Cadd9 | |A   Asus2 |
To be fated   to telling on - ly lies.

Chorus 1

         ||C |D |G |
But my dreams,   they aren't as empty
         |C |D |E |
As my conscience seems to be.
         |Bm | |C |
I have hours   only lone - ly.
                  |D |Dsus4   D |Asus2 | | ||
My love is ven - geance   that's never free.

Verse 2

Em |G |D |Dsus4   D
No one knows what it's like   to feel these feel - ings
          |Cadd9 | |Asus2 | |
Like I do,   and I blame you.
Em |G |D |Dsus4   D
No one bites back as hard   on their anger.
         |Cadd9 |Asus2 |
None of my pain and woe   can show through.

Chorus 2   *Repeat Chorus 1*

Interlude 1   E |Bm   A |E |Bm   A ‖

Bridge

E |Bm   A |E
  When my fist clench - es, crack it open
        |Bm   G |D
Before I use   it and lose my cool.
        |Bm A |D
When I smile,   tell me some bad   news
        |Bm   A |E |Bm   A |
Before I laugh and act like a fool.
E |Bm   A |E
  If I swal - low an - ything e - vil,
        |Bm   G |D
Put your fin - ger down   my throat.
        |Bm   A |D
And if I shiv - er, please give me a blanket.
        |Bm   A   ‖
Keep me warm;   let me wear your coat.

Interlude 2   *Repeat Interlude 1*

Guitar Solo |B |G   D   ‖:Bm |A   G   D   :‖
                    |B |B/A   ‖

Outro

Em |G |D |Dsus4 D
No one knows what it's like   to be the bad man,
           |Cadd9 | |Asus2 | ‖
To be the sad man   behind   blue eyes.

Happy Jack

Words and Music by
Peter Townshend

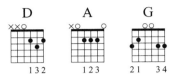

Intro | D | | |

Verse 1
‖D A |D |
Happy Jack wasn't old but he was a man.
| A |D | |
He lived in the sand at the Isle of Man.

Verse 2
‖D A |D |
The kids would all sing, he would sing the wrong key.
| A |D | ‖
So they rode on his head in their furry donkey.

Interlude 1 | D | | |

Chorus 1
‖G
The kids can't hurt Jack.
|A
They try, try, try.
|G
They drop things on his back
|A | |
And lie, lie, lie, lie, lie.

Verse 3

```
   ‖D                        A │D       |
They couldn't stop Jack and the wa - ters lapping
   |                             A   │D        ‖
Then they couldn't prevent Jack from feelin' happy.
```

Interlude 2

```
|A        |D        |A        |D        |
|A        |D        |A        |D        |
```

Verse 4

```
      ‖D                      A │D       |
But they couldn't stop Jack or the wa - ters lapping.
   |                             A   │D        ‖
Then they couldn't prevent Jack from feelin' happy.
```

Interlude 3

```
|A        |D        |A        |D        |
|G        |A   D │G        |A        |
|         |        |        ‖
```

Chorus 2

```
G
Kids couldn't hurt Jack.
   |A
They try, try, try.
   |G
They drop things on his back
   |A        |        |
And lie, lie, lie, lie, lie.
```

Verse 5

```
   ‖D                      A  │D       |
They couldn't stop Jack or the waters lapping
   |                             A   │D        ‖
Then they couldn't prevent Jack from feelin' happy.
```

Outro

```
|D        |        ‖
```

I Can't Explain

Words and Music by
Peter Townshend

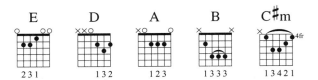

Intro

‖: E   D |A   E :‖
| D |A   E

Verse 1

        ‖E   D |A   E
How I feel inside… (Can't ex - plain.)
      | D |A   E
It's a certain kind… (Can't ex - plain.)
      | D |A   E
I feel hot and cold. (Can't ex - plain.)
        | D |B   E   ‖
Yeah, down in my soul, yeah. (Can't ex - plain.)

Interlude 1

E D |A   E
    I said… (Can't ex - plain.)
       | D |A   E   ‖
I'm feelin' good now, yeah, but… (Can't ex - plain.)

Verse 2

E   D |A   E
Dizzy in the head and I'm ___ feelin' blue.
    | D |A   E
The things you say, well, maybe they're true.
    | D |A   E
I'm gettin' funny dreams a - gain and again.
    | D B | ‖
I know what it means but,

Chorus 1

E |C#m
Can't explain. I think it's love.

   |A |B
Try to say it to you when I feel blue.

Interlude 2

‖E   D |A   E
But I can't explain, ___ (Can't ex - plain.)

| D |A   E   ‖
Yeah, hear what I'm say - in', girl. (Can't ex - plain.)

Guitar Solo 1

‖:E   D |A   E :‖

Verse 3

E   D |A   E
Dizzy in the head and I'm ___ feelin' bad.

| D |A   E
The things you said got ___ me really mad.

| D |A   E
I'm gettin' funny dreams a - gain and again.

| D   B | ‖
I know what it means but,

Chorus 2

Repeat Chorus 1

Interlude 3

‖E   D |A   E
But I can't explain. ___ (Can't explain.)

| D |A   E   ‖
Forgive me one more time ___ now. (Can't ex - plain.)

Guitar Solo 2

‖:E   D |A   E :‖ *Play 4 times*

Outro

E D |A   E | D
      Said I can't explain ___ it.

     |A   E | D
You drive me out of my mind.

     |A   E | D
Yeah, I'm the worryn' kind, ___ babe.

   |A   E   ‖
I said I can't explain.

I Can See for Miles

Words and Music by
Peter Townshend

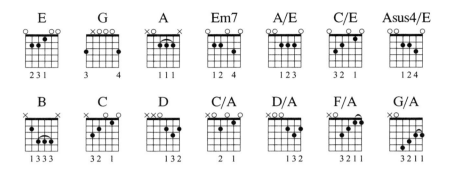

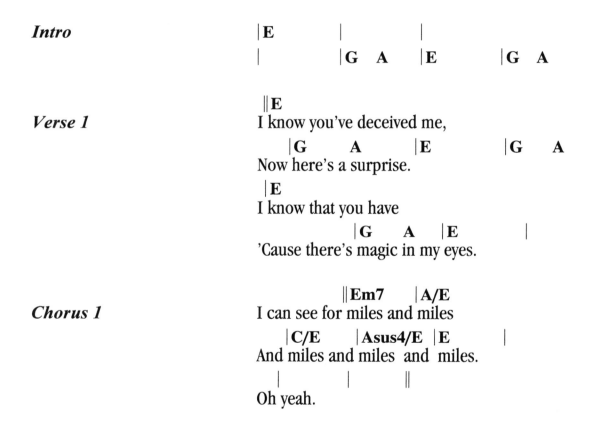

Intro

|E | |

| |G   A |E |G   A

Verse 1

‖E
I know you've deceived me,

  |G   A |E |G   A
Now here's a surprise.

 |E
I know that you have

          |G   A |E |
'Cause there's magic in my eyes.

Chorus 1

        ‖Em7 |A/E
I can see for miles and miles

   |C/E |Asus4/E |E |
And miles and miles and miles.

   | | ‖
Oh yeah.

Verse 2

E |G   A
  If you think that I don't know a - bout
           |E |G   A |E
The little tricks you play
                             |G
And never see you when de - liberately
     A |E
You put things in my way,
        |A
Well, here's a poke at you,
        |B
You're gonna choke on it too.
        |A
You're gonna lose that smile,
 |B |
Be - cause all the while,

Chorus 2

               ‖A   B |E
I can see for miles and miles.
           |A   B |E
I can see for miles and miles.
           |Em7 |A/E
I can see for miles and miles
 |C/E |Asus4/E |E |
And miles and miles and miles.
 | | ‖
Oh yeah.

Verse 3

E |G
  You took advantage of my trust in you
      A |E |G   A |E
When I was so far away.
                |
I saw you holding lots of other guys
              | |
And now you've got the nerve to say
  |A
That you still want me.
 |B
Well, that's as may be,
   |A
But you gotta stand trial,
 |B |
Be - cause all the while,

Chorus 3

Repeat Chorus 2

Interlude

|E |G   A   G |E |G   A   G |
|E |G   A |E | | |

Verse 4

‖E
I know you've deceived me,

| | |G   A
Now here's a surprise.

|E
I know that you have

| | |
'Cause there's magic in my eyes.

Chorus 4   *Repeat Chorus 1*

Verse 5

A |C
   The Eiffel Tower and the Taj Mahal
      D |A |C   D |A
Are mine to see on clear days.
                             |C
You thought that I would need a crystal ball
      D |A |
To see right through the haze.
                 |D
Well, here's a poke at you,
                 |E
You're gonna choke on it too.
                 |D
You're gonna lose that smile,
      |E |
Be - cause all the while,

Chorus 5

                 ‖D   E |A
I can see for miles and miles.
                 |D   E |A
I can see for miles and miles.
                   |C/A |D/A
I can see for miles and miles
      |F/A |G/A |
And miles and miles and miles
      | | |A | | |
And miles and miles and miles.

Outro

                   ‖:D   E |A   :‖
I can see for miles and miles. I can see for   *Repeat & fade*

20

Join Together

Words and Music by
Peter Townshend

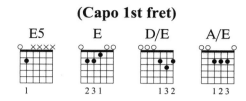

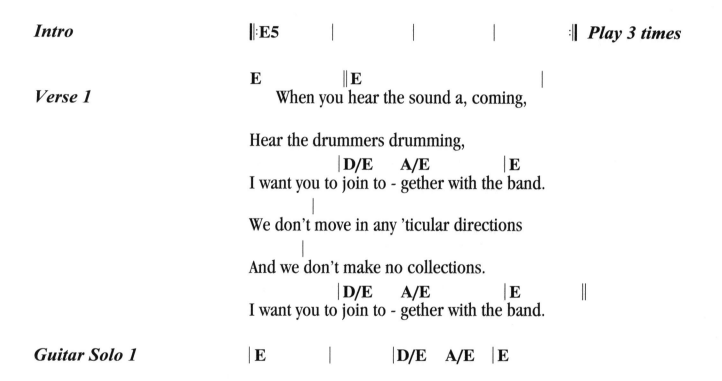

Intro   ‖: E5 | | :‖   ***Play 3 times***

Verse 1

E   ‖E |
      When you hear the sound a, coming,

Hear the drummers drumming,
       |D/E   A/E |E
I want you to join to - gether with the band.

     |
We don't move in any 'ticular directions

     |
And we don't make no collections.
       |D/E   A/E |E   ‖
I want you to join to - gether with the band.

Guitar Solo 1 |E | |D/E   A/E |E

Verse 2

          ‖**E**
Do you really think I care

        |
What you read or what you wear?

          |**D/E**   **A/E** |**E**
I want you to join to - gether with the band.

        |
There's a million ways to laugh,

        |
And ev'ry one's a path.

          |**D/E**   **A/E** |**E**   ‖
Come on and join to - gether with the band.

Guitar Solo 2 |**E** | |**D/E** **A/E** |**E**

Chorus 1

         ‖**E**
Ev'rybody, join together,

        |
I want you to join together.

                  |**D/E**   **A/E** |**E**
Well, come on and join to - gether with the band.

        |
We need you to join together,

        |
Come on and join together,

         |**D/E**   **A/E** |**E**   ‖
Come on and join to - gether with the band.

Interlude   ‖:**E5** | | | :‖

Verse 3

        E
You don't have to pay,

        |
And you can follow or lead the way.

          |**D/E**   **A/E** |**E**
I want you to join to - gether with the band.

        |
We don't know where we're going,

        |
But the season's ripe for knowing.

          |**D/E**   **A/E** |**E**   ‖
I want you to join to - gether with the band.

Synth Solo |E | |D/E   A/E |E

Verse 4
                                                ‖E
It's the singer, not the song
                                    |
That makes the music move along.
                                            |D/E   A/E |E
I want you to join to - gether with the band.
                                    |
This is the biggest band you'll find,
                                    |
It's as deep as it is wide.
                                            |D/E   A/E |E
Come on and join to - gether with the band.
                                                ‖
Hey, hey, hey, hey, hey,

Chorus 2
E | |
Hey.   Oh, ev'rybody come on, ___ come on,   come on and join us.
(Join together,   join   together.)
D/E   A/E |E
Join to - gether with the band.
                                    | |
We need you to join together, ev'rybody come on. Hey, hey, hey
D/E   A/E |E   ‖
Join to - gether with the band.

Outro ‖:E5 | :‖ *Repeat & fade*

Love, Reign O'er Me

Words and Music by
Peter Townshend

(Capo 1st fret)

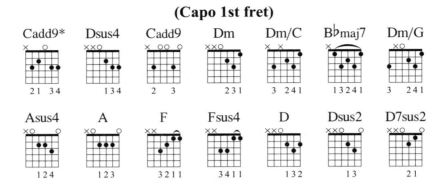

Intro |**Cadd9*** | | |

Verse 1

‖**Dsus4** | | |
Only love   can make it rain

|**Cadd9** | | |
The way the beach   is kissed by the sea.

|**Dsus4** | | |
Only love   can make it rain

|**Cadd9** | | | ‖
Like the sweat of lov - ers   laying in the fields.

Chorus 1

Dm | | |
Love,

Dm/C |**B♭maj7** | |**Dm/G** | |
Reign o'er   me.

Dm | | |
Love,

Dm/C |**B♭maj7** | |**Dm/G** | |
Reign o'er   me,   reign o'er me,

|**Asus4** | |**A** | |
Rain on me.

Verse 2

```
  ‖Dsus4    |                    |                    |
Only  love        can bring the rain
                  |Cadd9    |              |              |
That makes you yearn        to the sky.
      |Dsus4    |                    |                    |
Only love           can bring the rain
                  |Cadd9    |              |         |         ‖
That falls like tears        from on high.
```

Chorus 2

```
Dm           |              |              |
Love,
        Dm/C   |B♭maj7    |                        |Dm/G
Reign o'er      me,                reign o'er me,
                         |              |
Reign o'er me.
Dm           |              |              |
Love,
        Dm/C   |B♭maj7 |
Reign o'er      me, reign o'er me,
      |Dm/G    |              |Asus4    |           |A        |        ‖
Reign o'er me.
```

Bridge

```
F          |Fsus4              |F
   On the dry and dusty road,
                    |Fsus4              |F
The nights we spent apart alone,
              |Fsus4
I need to get back home
   |D          |Dsus4    |D          |Dsus4      |F
To cool, cool rain.
                         |Fsus4              |F
I can't sleep and I lay and I think,
                    |Fsus4              |F
The night is hot and black as ink,
                    |Fsus4
Woo, oh, God I need a drink
   |D          |Dsus4    |Dsus2    |Dsus4      ‖
Of cool, cool rain.
```

Guitar Solo

	F		Fsus4		F		Fsus4	
	F		Fsus4		D		Dsus4	
	Dsus2				F		Fsus4	
	F		Fsus4		F		Fsus4	
	D		Dsus4		Dsus2		Dsus4	
|Cadd9							
|Dsus4							
	Cadd9						‖

Chorus 3

Dm | | |
Love,

     Dm/C |B♭maj7 |
Reign o'er   me.

            |**Dm/G** | |
Reign o'er me, o - ver me, over me,   oh!

Dm | | |
Love,

     Dm/C |B♭maj7 |
Reign o'er   me,

    | |**Dm/G** | |
Oh, ___ oh, oh, oh,   on me.

|**Asus4** | |**A** | | |
| | | | ‖ |

Outro

|**Dsus4** | | | |
 Love!

| |**D7sus2** | | ‖ |

The Magic Bus

Words and Music by
Peter Townshend

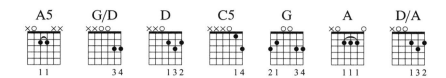

Intro

```
‖: N.C.    |            :‖ A5    |            |
|          |G/D  D  |A       |C5  G/D  |
|A         |C5  G/D |A       |G/D  D   |
|A     G   |    D   A   |C    G/D  ‖
```

Verse 1

```
A         |C5  G/D    D   |
```
Ev'ry day I get in the queue
```
A         |G     D    |
```
(Too much, the magic bus.)
```
   |A                |C5  G/D    D   |
```
To get on the bus that takes ___ me ___ to you.
```
A         |G     D    |
```
(Too much, the magic bus.)
```
A         |G/D  D   |A       |
```
I'm so nervous, I ___ just sit and smile.
```
          |G     D    |
```
(Too much, the magic bus.)
```
          |A        |G/D    D    |
```
Your house ___ is only an - other mile.
```
A         |G     D    ‖
```
(Too much, the magic bus.)

Verse 2

```
A                      |C5    G/D   D   |
Thank you, driver, for getting me    here.
   A          |G         D
(Too much, the magic bus.)
        |A                 |C5    G/D   D   |
You'll be an inspector, have ___ no___   fear.
   A            |G      D      |
(Too much, the magic bus.)
A                  |G/D    D
I don't wanna cause ___ no fuss,
   A            |G      D      |
(Too much, the magic bus.)
    |A              G/D   D    |
But can I buy your magic bus?
   A            |G      D      ||
(Too much, the magic bus.)
```

Interlude 1

```
|| A5        |           | N.C.      |          |
   No!
| A5         |           |           |    D5    |
| A          |           |           | C5  G/D  ||
```

Verse 3

```
A                      |G/D    D  |
I don't care how much ___ I pay.
A          |G       D
   (Ride the magic bus.)
        |A              |G/D     D   |
I wanna drive my bus to my baby each day.
A         |G       D  ‖
   (Ride the magic bus.)
```

Interlude 2

```
|A        |C5   G/D |A        |C5   G/D |
A   |         |N.C.   |         |        |      |
     I want it, I want it, I want it, I want it, you can't have it.
   |     A5    |                      ‖
I want ___ it, I want it, I want…
```

Verse 4

```
N.C.                    |        |A5    |        |
Thruppence and sixpence every day.
N.C.            |        |A5    |        |
Just to drive to my baby.
N.C.                    |        |A     D/A | A
Thruppence and sixpence each day.
       D/A |    A    D/A    A    D/A    |A  D/A  |G/D       ‖
'Cause I    drive my ba - by every way.
```

Outro

```
A   |C5       G/D    |
   Oh, magic bus.
‖: A          |G/D   D  :‖
   (Magic bus.)              *Play 10 times*
‖: A          |G/D   D  :‖  *Repeat and fade (w/ voc. ad lib.)*
```

My Generation

Words and Music by
Peter Townshend

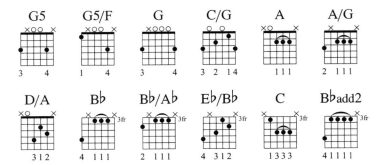

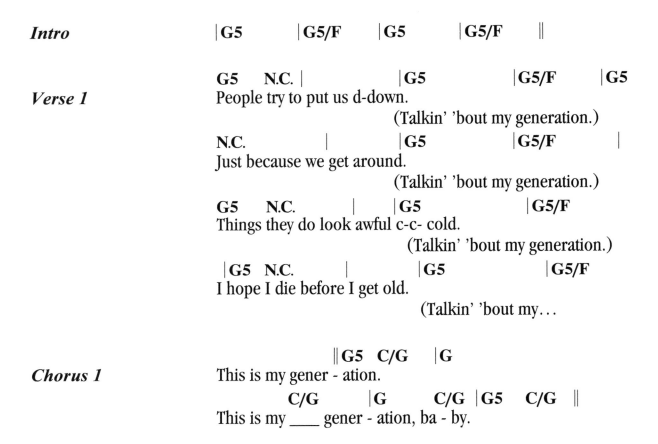

Intro | **G5** | **G5/F** | **G5** | **G5/F** ||

Verse 1

G5   **N.C.** | | **G5** | **G5/F** | **G5**
People try to put us d-down.

                (Talkin' 'bout my generation.)

N.C. | | **G5** | **G5/F** |
Just because we get around.

                (Talkin' 'bout my generation.)

G5   **N.C.** | **G5** | **G5/F**
Things they do look awful c-c- cold.

                (Talkin' 'bout my generation.)

| **G5**   **N.C.** | **G5** | **G5/F**
I hope I die before I get old.

                (Talkin' 'bout my…

Chorus 1

|| **G5**   **C/G** | **G**
This is my gener - ation.

       C/G | **G**   **C/G** | **G5**   **C/G** ||
This is my ___ gener - ation, ba - by.

Verse 2

G5   N.C. | |G5 |G5/F |
Why don't you all f-fade ____ away.
                  (Talkin' 'bout my generation.)

G5   N.C. | |G5 |G5/F |
Don't try and dig what we all s-s-say.
                  (Talkin' 'bout my generation.)

G5 N.C. | |G5 |G5/F
Not tryin' to cause a big s-s-sen - sation,
                (Talkin' 'bout my generation.)

  |G5 N.C. | |G5 |G5/F
I'm just talkin' 'bout my g-g-g-gen - eration.
                (Talkin' 'bout my generation.)

Chorus 2

      ‖G5   C/G |G
My gener - ation.

        C/G |G   C/G |G   C/G ‖
This is my genera - tion, ba - by.

Guitar/Bass Solo

‖: G5 N.C. | |G   C/G |G5 C/G :‖ *Play 4 times*
|G   C/G |G5   C/G |G   C/G |G5   ‖

Verse 3

A   N.C. | |A |A/G
Why don't you all f-fade away.
           (Talkin' 'bout my generation.)

 |A   N.C. | |A |A/G |
Yeah, don't try and d-dig what we all s - s - s - s - s - say.
               (Talkin' 'bout my generation.)

A N.C. | |A |A/G
Not tryin' to cause big sen - sation,
           (Talkin' 'bout my generation.)

 |A N.C. | |A |A/G
Just talk - in' 'bout my g-generation.
             (Talkin' 'bout my...

Chorus 3

     ‖A   D/A |
Baby, my gener - ation,

        |A |D/A |A
This is my gener - ation, baby.

  |D/A |A
My, my,   gener - ation.

  D/A | |B♭
My, ___ my, ooh, my, my.

 |B♭/A♭ |B♭ |B♭/A♭   ‖
My, my, my generation.

Verse 4

Bb   N.C. | |Bb |Bb/Ab |

People try to put us down,

                    (Talkin' 'bout my generation.)

Bb N.C. | |Bb |Bb/Ab |

   Just because we g-g-g-get around.

                     (Talkin' 'bout my generation.)

Bb   N.C. | |Bb   Eb/Bb

Things they do look aw - ful c-c-cold.

                (Talkin' 'bout ___ my generation.)

 |Bb N.C. | |Bb |Eb/Bb

Yeah, I hope I die before I get old.

              (Talkin' 'bout my generation.)

Chorus 4

       ‖ Bb |Eb/Bb

My gener - ation,

         |Bb |Eb/Bb

This is my gener - ation, baby.

   |Bb |Eb/Bb

My, ___ my, my,

       |Bb |Eb/Bb   ‖

My, my, gener - ation, genera - tion.

Guitar Solo

‖:C |Bbadd2 |C |Bbadd2 :‖

|C | Bbadd2 |C | Bbadd2 |

|C |Bbadd2 | | |

 C | Bbadd2 |

(Talkin' 'bout my gener - ation.)

 C | Bbadd2 ‖

(Talkin' 'bout my gener - ation.)

Outro

‖:C |Bbadd2 :‖

 (Talkin' 'bout my generation.)   *Repeat and fade w/ lead Voc. ad lib.*

Pictures of Lily

Words and Music by
Peter Townshend

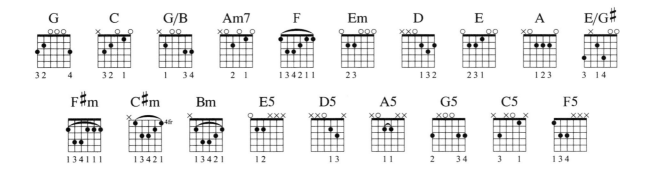

Intro |G | ||

Verse 1

C   G/B |Am7   G |
I used to wake up in the morning.

             | |C
I used to feel so bad.

        G/B |Am7   G |
I got so sick of having sleepless nights.

            |
I went and told my dad.

       |Am7   G |F   Em |Am7
He said, "Son, now here's some little some - things,"

           G | |C
And stuck them on my wall.

      G/B |Am7
And now my night seem quite so lonely.

    G | | |
In fact I   don't feel bad at all.

       | ||
I don't feel bad at all.

Chorus 1

C   Em |
Pictures of Lily

Am7   G |F   Em |D   G |
Made my life ____ so wonderful.

C   Em |
Pictures of Lily

Am7   G |F   Em |D |E | ‖
Help me sleep at night.

Chorus 2

A   E/G♯ |
Pictures of Li - ly

F♯m   E |D   C♯m |Bm   E |
Solved my childhood prob - lem.

A   E/G♯ |
Pictures of Lil - y

F♯m   E |D |E | ‖
Helped me feel al - right.

Bridge

|E5   D5   E5 |

N.C. |E5   D5   E5 |
Pictures of Lily,

N.C. |A5   G5   A5 |
Lily, oh Lily.

N.C. |A5   G5   A5 |
Lily, oh Lily.

N.C. |D5   C5   D5 | C5   D5 |G5   F5   G5 | ‖
Pictures of Lily.

Verse 2

```
C               G/B           |Am7        G  |
    And then one day things were quite so fine,
                        |            |C
I fell in love with Lil - y.
              G/B           |Am7
I asked my dad where Lily I could find,
          G  |                     |          |Am7
He said, ___     "Son, now don't be silly.
          G              |F      Em  |Am7
She's been dead since nineteen twenty nine."
                              |G       |C
Oh, how I cried that night.
        G/B           |Am7      G  |
If only I'd been born in Lily's time,
                    |         |        ‖
It would appear al - right.
```

Chorus 3

```
C       Em     |
Pictures of Lily
Am7        G        |F     Em  |D   G  |
Made my life ___ so won - derful.
C       Em     |
Pictures of Lily
Am7    G    |F     Em  |D       |E    |        ‖
Help me sleep at night.
```

Chorus 4

```
A             E/G♯
    But me and Lily
        |F♯m   E   |D    C♯m  |Bm   E    |A
Are to - gether in my dream.
        E/G♯          |F♯m          E  |D        |
And I ask you, "Hey, Mister, have you ever seen
E5        D5   E5  N.C. ‖
Pictures of Lil - y?"
```

Pinball Wizard

Words and Music by
Peter Townshend

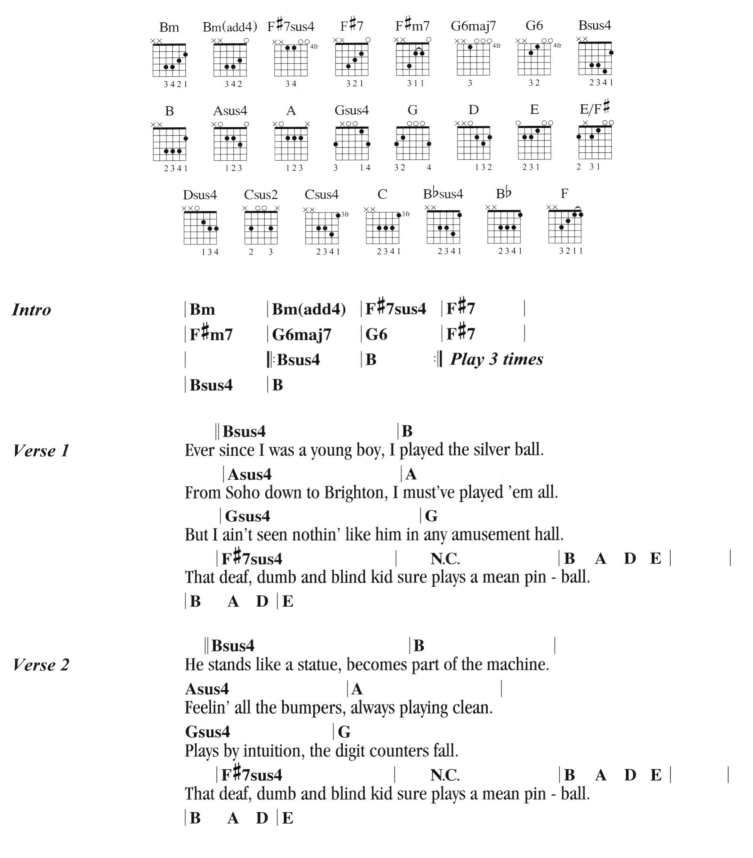

Intro

Bm	Bm(add4)	F#7sus4	F#7
F#m7	G6maj7	G6	F#7
	‖: Bsus4	B	:‖ *Play 3 times*
Bsus4	B

Verse 1

‖ Bsus4 | B
Ever since I was a young boy, I played the silver ball.
        | Asus4 | A
From Soho down to Brighton, I must've played 'em all.
        | Gsus4 | G
But I ain't seen nothin' like him in any amusement hall.
        | F#7sus4 | N.C. | B A D E | |
That deaf, dumb and blind kid sure plays a mean pin - ball.
| B   A D | E

Verse 2

‖ Bsus4 | B |
He stands like a statue, becomes part of the machine.
Asus4 | A |
Feelin' all the bumpers, always playing clean.
Gsus4 | G
Plays by intuition, the digit counters fall.
        | F#7sus4 | N.C. | B A D E | |
That deaf, dumb and blind kid sure plays a mean pin - ball.
| B   A D | E

Chorus 1

```
           ‖E    E/F♯ B
He's a pin - ball    wizard.
           |E     E/F♯ B
There has to be  a   twist.
      |E    E/F♯  B          |G            |D   Dsus4 |D        ‖
A pin - ball    wizard's got such a supple wrist.
```

Bridge

```
      D          Csus2     |D       Csus2      |
How do you think he does ___ it? (I don't know.)
      D          Csus2 |D        ‖
What makes him  so  good?
```

Verse 3

```
      Bsus4                  |B
Ain't got no distractions, can't hear no buzzers and bells.
      |Asus4              |A                |
Don't see no lights a flashin', plays by sense of smell.
      Gsus4            |G
Always gets a replay, never seen him fall.
      |F♯7sus4            |  N.C.          |B   A   D   E |          |
That deaf, dumb and blind kid sure plays a mean pin-ball.
      |B    A   D |E
```

Chorus 2

```
      ‖E       E/F♯ B    E |     E/F♯ B
I thought  I     was  the Bally table  king
      |E  E/F♯ B          |G            |D Dsus4 D |        ‖
But I   just    handed my pinball crown to him.
```

Interlude

```
‖:Dsus4      |D        :‖ Play 3 times
|Dsus4       |D
```

Verse 4

```
      ‖Dsus4          |D
Even on my fav'rite table, he can beat my best.
      |Csus4            |C
His dis - ciples lead him in and he just does the rest.
      |B♭sus4          |B♭
He's got crazy flipper fingers, never seen him fall.
      |Asus4              |  N.C.          |D   C   F ‖
That deaf, dumb and blind kid sure plays a mean pin - ball.
```

Outro

```
‖:B♭sus4     |              :‖ Repeat and fade
```

The Real Me

Words and Music by
Peter Townshend

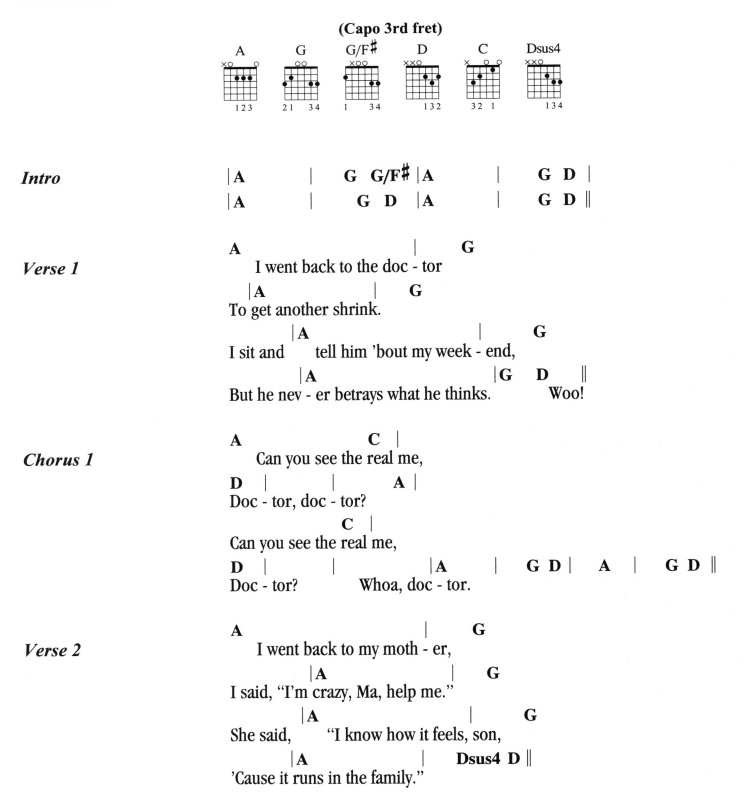

(Capo 3rd fret)

A   G   G/F#   D   C   Dsus4

Intro

|A | G G/F# |A | G D |

|A | G D |A | G D ‖

Verse 1

|A | G
     I went back to the doc - tor

|A | G
To get another shrink.

        |A | G
I sit and   tell him 'bout my week - end,

        |A |G   D   ‖
But he nev - er betrays what he thinks.   Woo!

Chorus 1

|A   C |
     Can you see the real me,

D | | A |
Doc - tor, doc - tor?

         C |
Can you see the real me,

D | | |A | G D | A | G D ‖
Doc - tor?   Whoa, doc - tor.

Verse 2

|A | G
     I went back to my moth - er,

        |A | G
I said, "I'm crazy, Ma, help me."

        |A | G
She said,   "I know how it feels, son,

        |A | Dsus4 D ‖
'Cause it runs in the family."

Chorus 2

A   C |
Can you see the real me,
D | | A |
Moth - er, moth - er?
                       C |
Can you see the real me,
D | |
Moth - er?

Bridge

              ‖A   C |
Whoa, moth - er.
             Dsus4 | D |
Can you see?   Can you see?
                |A
Can you see the real me?
        C | Dsus4 |
Can you see? Can you see
             D | ‖
The real me, the real me, the real me?

Interlude 1 |A   C | Dsus4| |D   ‖

Verse 3

A   N.C. |
Cracks between the pav - ing stones
    | | |
Like rivers of flowing veins.
                |
Strange people who know me
        | |
Peeping from be - hind ev'ry window pane.

Verse 4

    ‖A | G
The girl I used to love
    |A | G |A
Lives in this yellow house.
      | G
Yesterday she passed me by;
      |A |G D   ‖
She doesn't want to know me now.   Whoa!

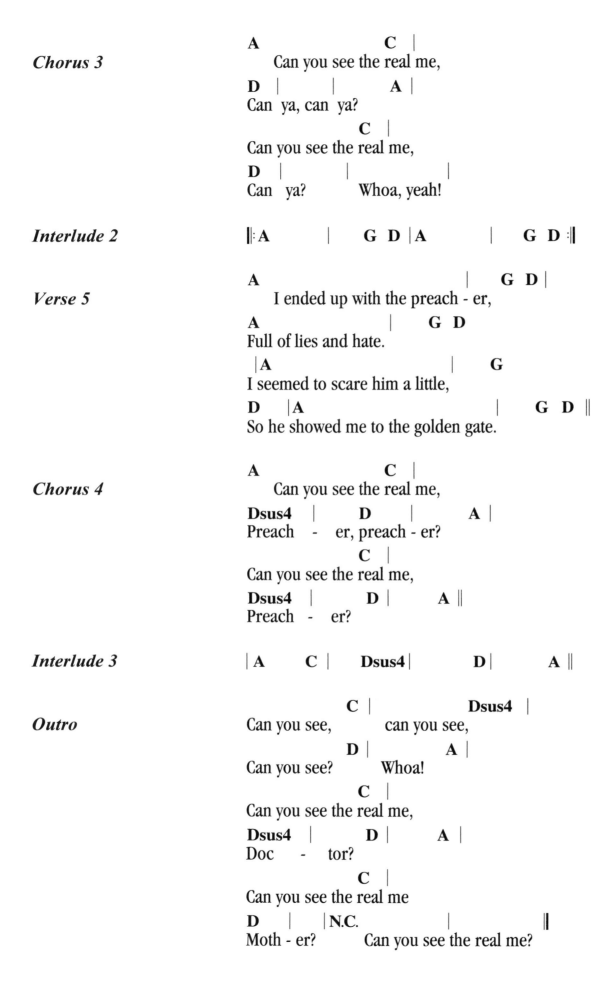

Chorus 3

```
         A                C  |
             Can you see the real me,
D  |          |        A  |
Can  ya, can  ya?
                      C  |
Can you see the real me,
D  |          |                |
Can   ya?        Whoa, yeah!
```

Interlude 2

```
‖: A          |      G  D | A          |      G  D :‖
```

Verse 5

```
A                              |      G  D |
         I ended up with the preach - er,
A                  |      G  D
Full of lies and hate.
 | A                    |      G
I seemed to scare him a little,
D  | A                          |      G  D ‖
So he showed me to the golden gate.
```

Chorus 4

```
A                C  |
         Can you see the real me,
Dsus4  |      D      |      A  |
Preach   -   er, preach - er?
                      C  |
Can you see the real me,
Dsus4  |      D  |      A  ‖
Preach   -   er?
```

Interlude 3

```
| A      C  |      Dsus4 |          D  |          A  ‖
```

Outro

```
                   C  |              Dsus4  |
Can you see,        can you see,
                   D  |          A  |
Can you see?        Whoa!
                   C  |
Can you see the real me,
Dsus4  |      D  |      A  |
Doc    -   tor?
                   C  |
Can you see the real me
D      |   | N.C.          |                ‖
Moth - er?        Can you see the real me?
```

The Seeker

Words and Music by
Peter Townshend

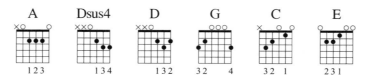

Intro

|A   Dsus4 D |A   Dsus4 D |G C |
| G |A   Dsus4 D |A   Dsus4 D ‖

Verse 1

          A   Dsus4 D |A
      I've looked under chairs,
                                   Dsus4 D
I've looked under tables.
 |A   Dsus4 D
I tried to find the key
 |A
To fifty million fables.

Chorus 1

       Dsus4 D   ‖D   C |D
They call   me the seeker.
                            |A Dsus4 D |A |D C
I've been searchin' low and high.
                         | G
I won't get to get what I'm after
                   |A Dsus4 D |A   D ‖
'Till the day I die.

Verse 2

          A   **Dsus4 D** |**A**
     I asked Bobby Dylan.

                       Dsus4 D |**A**
I asked the Beatles.

I asked Timothy Leary,
Dsus4 D |**A**
But   he   couldn't help me either.

Chorus 2

         C   ‖**D**   **C** |**D**
They call me the seeker.

                   C |**A**   **Dsus4 D** |**A**   **Dsus4 D** |**G** **C**
I've been searchin' low and high.

                                | **G**
I won't get to get what I'm after

                  |**A**   **Dsus4 D** |**A**   **G**   ‖
'Till the day I die.

Bridge 1

  D   **Dsus4 D** |
     People tend to hate me,

                    Dsus4
'Cause I never smile.
D |**A**   **Asus4 A** | **Asus4 A** |**D**
As I ransack their homes, they wanna shake   my hand.

                       Dsus4 D | **Dsus4**
Focus in on nowhere,   in - vestigatin' miles.
D |**E** | **N.C.**   ‖
I'm a seeker, I'm a really desperate man.

Guitar Solo

```
|A     D |A      D |A      D |A      D |
|         |         |A      D |A      D |G  C
                              |  G
```
I won't get to get what I'm after
```
                     |A     D |A     D ||
```
'Till the day I die.

Bridge 2

```
D                          Dsus4   D  |
```
I learned how to raise my voice, ____ in an - ger.
```
Dsus4  D |A               Asus4  A |        Asus4
```
Yeah,   but look at my face, ain't this   a   smile?
```
A   |D                Dsus4
```
I'm   happy when life's good
```
D  |                Dsus4
```
And when it's bad, I cry.
```
D    |E                        |  N.C.      ||
```
I've got values but I don't know how or why.

Verse 3

```
A                    Dsus4  D |A
```
   I'm lookin' for me,
```
                        Dsus4  D
```
You're lookin' for you.
```
      |A
```
We're lookin' at each other
```
Dsus4  D |A
```
And   we don't know what to do.

Chorus 3

```
        Dsus4  D ||D       C |D
```
They call me   the seeker.
```
                    C          |A   Dsus4 D |A   Dsus4 D |G   C
```
I've been searchin' low and high.
```
                         |  G
```
I won't get to get what I'm after
```
               |A   Dsus4 D |G  C   G   A   ||
```
'Till the day I die.

Squeeze Box

Words and Music by
Peter Townshend

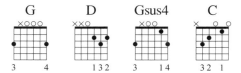

Intro

```
|G    D   |G    D   |G    D   |G    D   |
|G  Gsus4 G  Gsus4 G  |    Gsus4 G  Gsus4 G  |
|    Gsus4 G  Gsus4 G  |    Gsus4 G  Gsus4
```

Verse 1

```
G    ‖        Gsus4 G      Gsus4
Ma - ma's got      a squeeze box
G    |        Gsus4 G
She wears on her       chest,
         Gsus4 G |      Gsus4 G
And when ____ Daddy comes  home
        Gsus4 G|      Gsus4 G
He nev - er gets no _____ rest.
Gsus4 G  |D            |
'Cause  she's playin' all night
            |C            |
And the music's all right.
            |D
Ma - ma's got a squeeze box,
            |C                ‖
Dad - dy never sleeps at night.
```

Interlude 1

```
|G  Gsus4 G  Gsus4 G  |    Gsus4 G  Gsus4 G  |
|    Gsus4 G  Gsus4 G  |    Gsus4 G
```

Verse 2

Gsus4 ‖G　　　Gsus4　G
Well, the　　kids don't _____ eat

Gsus4　G |　　　Gsus4　G
And　　the dog can't _____ sleep,

　　　　　Gsus4　G |　　　Gsus4　G
There's no　　es - cape from the　　music

Gsus4　G |　　　　Gsus4　G
In　　the whole damn _____ street.

Gsus4　G　|D　　　　　|
'Cause　she's playin' all night

　　　|C　　　　　　|
And the music's all right.

　　　|D
Ma - ma's got a squeeze box,

　　　|C　　　　　　‖
Dad - dy never sleeps at night.

Interlude 2

|G　Gsus4　G　Gsus4　G　|　　Gsus4　G　Gsus4　G　|
|　　Gsus4　G　Gsus4　G　|　　Gsus4　G

Chorus 1

　　　Gsus4　G ‖G　Gsus4　G
She goes _____ in　and　　out

Gsus4　G　|　Gsus4　G
And　　in ___ and　　out

Gsus4　G　|　Gsus4　G
And　　in ___ and　　out

Gsus4　G |　　Gsus4　G
And　　in ___ and　　out,

Gsus4　G　|D　　　　　　|
'Cause　she's playin' all night

　　　|C　　　　　|
And the music's all right.

　　　|D
Ma - ma's got a squeeze box,

　　　|C　　　　　　　‖
Dad - dy never sleeps at night.

Interlude 3 |G Gsus4 G Gsus4 G | Gsus4 G Gsus4 G |
                 Gsus4 G Gsus4 G   Gsus4 G

                          Gsus4 G ‖ G |
Bridge   She goes _____ squeeze me.
                                 | |
                 Come on and squeeze me.
                                   |D |
                 Come on and tease me like you do,
                     |C |
                 I'm so in love with you.
                     |D
                 Ma - ma's got a squeeze box,
                     |C |G | ‖
                 Dad - dy never sleeps at night.

Banjo Solo   ‖:G   Gsus4 G Gsus4 G | Gsus4 G Gsus4 G :‖
                 |D | |
                 |C | |
                 |D |C |
                 |G   Gsus4 G Gsus4 G | Gsus4 G

Chorus 2   *Repeat Chorus 1*

Outro |G   C   G   C |G   C   G   ‖

Substitute

Words and Music by
Peter Townshend

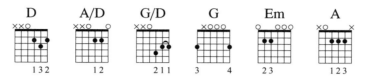

Intro | D   A/D   G/D | D | A/D   G/D | D |
             | | | | ||

Verse 1

D |G |D | |
You think we look pretty good togeth - er.

             |G |D |
You think my shoes are made of leath - er.

Pre-Chorus 1

‖ Em |
But I'm a substitute for an - other guy.

| |
I look pretty tall, but my heels are high.

| |
The simple things you see are all complicated.

| | |
I look pretty young, but I'm just backdated,

A | ‖
Yeah.

Chorus 1

D   A/D   G/D | D
Substi - tute your lies   for fact.

| A/D   G/D | D
I see right through your plas - tic mac.

| A/D   G/D | D
I look all white,   but my   dad was black.

| A/D   G/D | D | | ‖
My fine-looking suit is real - ly   made out of   sack.

Verse 2

D | G | D |
  I was born with a plastic spoon in my mouth.

| | G
The north side of my town faced east,

              | D |
And the east was fac - ing south.

Pre-Chorus 2

           ‖ Em |
And now you dare to look me in the eye.

      | |
Those crocodile tears are what you cry.

    | |
It's a genuine problem; you won't try

   | |
To work it out at all. Just pass it by,

    | A | ‖
Pass it by.

Chorus 2

D   A/D   G/D | D |
Substi - tute   me for him.

      A/D   G/D | D |
Substi - tute my   Coke for gin.

      A/D   G/D | D
Substi - tute you   for my mum.

| A/D G/D | D | | ‖
At least I'll get my   washing done.

Interlude 1	|D	|G	|D	|	|
	|	|G	|D	|	||

Pre-Chorus 3   *Repeat Pre-Chorus 1*

Interlude 2

|D	A/D	G/D|	D	|	A/D	G/D|	D	|
|	A/D	G/D|	D	|	A/D	G/D|	D	|
|		|		||				

Verse 3   *Repeat Verse 2*

Pre-Chorus 4   *Repeat Pre-Chorus 2*

Chorus 3

```
D       A/D   G/D|        D      |
Substi - tute           me for him.
         A/D   G/D|           D      |
Substi - tute   my      Coke for gin.
         A/D   G/D|        D      |
Substi - tute   you      for my  mum.
   |         A/D  G/D|        D      |
At least I'll get my       washing done.
```

Chorus 4   *Repeat Chorus 1*

Who Are You

Words and
Music by Peter Townshend

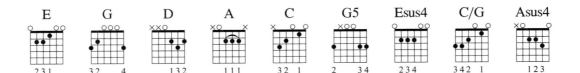

Intro

```
‖: E      |      |      |      :‖
|      |      |      | G  D ‖
```

Chorus 1

```
‖: E   D |      |
(Who are you?)
A    E A   E |        :‖ Play 4 times
(Who - o, who - o.)
```

Verse 1

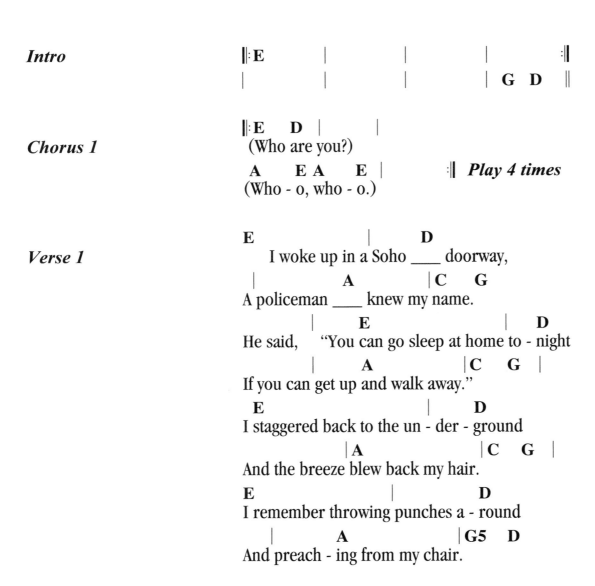

```
      E                 |      D
      I woke up in a Soho ___ doorway,
|           A        |C   G
A policeman ___ knew my name.
         |      E        | D
He said,   "You can go sleep at home to - night
         |      A        |C   G |
If you can get up and walk away."
      E                 | D
I staggered back to the un - der - ground
              |A        |C   G |
And the breeze blew back my hair.
      E                 | D
I remember throwing punches a - round
      |      A        |G5   D
And preach - ing from my chair.
```

Chorus 2

```
          C      ‖E   D   |            |
Well, who are you?
                  (Who are    you?)
     A    E A    E |
(Who - o, who - o.)
                  |     D  |            |
I really want to know.
                  (Who are    you?)
     A    E A    E |
(Who - o, who - o.)
                  |     D  |        |
Tell me who are you
                  (Who are    you?)
     A    E A    E |
(Who - o, who - o.)
                  |     D  |            |
'Cause I really want to know.
                  (Who are    you?)
     A    E A    E |          ‖
(Who - o, who - o.)
```

Verse 2

```
     E                     |   D
     I took the tube back out of town
     |    A              |C   G   |
Back to ___ the rolling pin.
     E                |    D
I felt a little like a dying ___ hound
     |      A             |C   G   |
With a streak of "Rin Tin Tin."
     E                |     D
I stretched back and I hiccupped,
          |     A          |C   G   |
And looked back on my busy day.
     E              |   D
E - leven hours in the tin pan,
          |    A             |G5   D
God, there's got to be another way.
```

Chorus 3

```
             C      ‖E   D   |          |
Well, who are you?
                  (Who are      you?)
      A    E A    E |
(Who - o, who - o.)
                  |      D   |          |
Oh, who are you?
                  (Who are      you?)
      A   E A   E |
(Who - o, who - o.)
                         |        D   |          |
C'mon, tell me who are you.
                         (Who are      you?)
      A    E A    E |
(Who - o, who - o.)
                         |        D   |          |
Oh, who the fuck are you?
                         (Who are      you?)
      A    E A    E |         ‖
(Who - o, who - o.)
```

Interlude

```
|A      G |     D  |        |       |E          |
|        |        |        |       |       |        |
‖:E      D |        |A E A E|              :‖ Play 3 times
|  Esus4  |  G  D  |  Esus4  |  G  D  |
|  Esus4  |  G  D  |  Esus4  |  G  D  ‖
Who                            are   you?
```

Bridge

```
‖:E          |       |       |
  Do, da, do, ___ da, do, da,
                  |            :‖ Play 5 times
Do, da, do, ___ da, do.
‖:E       |  G  D  |E          |  G  D :‖
```

Chorus 4

```
‖: E    D  |         |
  (Who are  you?)
       A    E A    E |              :‖ Play 3 times
  (Who - o, who - o.)
            D  |         |
  (Who are  you?)
       A    E A    E |
  (Who - o, who - o.)
                   |    D  |        |
  I really want to know.
                       (Who are      you?)
       A    E A    E |
  (Who - o, who - o.)
                   |      D  |          |
  I really want to know.
                       (Who are       you?)
       A     E A    E  |
  (Who - o, who - o.)
                       |        D  |          |
  C'mon, tell me who are you,
                          (Who are      you?)
       A    E A    E |
  (Who - o, who - o.)
                   |     D  |          |
  I really want to know.
                       (Who are       you?)
       A    E A    E |           ‖
  (Who - o, who - o.)
```

Verse 3

```
  E                         |      D
     I know there's a place you ___ walked
       |     A         |C    G  |
  Where love falls from the trees.
       E          |         D
  My heart is like a broken cup,
         |    A              |C    G  |
  I only feel right on my knees.
       E               |       D
  I spill out like a sew - er hole
         |    A              |C    G  |
  And still receive your kiss.
            E              |      D
  How can I measure up to any - one now,
         |    A              |G5    D
  After such a love as this?
```

        C   ‖**E** **D** | |

Well, who are you?

             (Who are   you?)

  A   **E A**   **E** |

(Who - o, who - o.)

                | **D** | |

C'mon, tell me who are you,

             (Who are   you?)

  A   **E A**   **E**|

(Who - o, who - o.)

               | **D** | |

Oh, I really want to know.

             (Who are   you?)

  A   **E A**   **E**|

(Who - o, who - o.)

              | **D** | |

Tell me, tell me who are you.

            (Who are   you?)

  A   **E A**   **E** |

(Who - o, who - o.)

            | **D** | |

C'mon, c'mon, oh, who.

          (Who are   you?)

  A   **E A**   **E**|

(Who - o, who - o.)

             | **D** | |

Ah, who the fuck are you?

           (Who are   you?)

  A   **E A**   **E** |

(Who - o, who - o.)

          | **D** | |

Who fuckin' who.

        (Who are   you?)

  A   **E A**   **E** |

(Who - o, who - o.)

            | **D** | |

Ah, tell me who are you.

           (Who are   you?)

  A | |**C/G** |

(Who.)   I really want to know.

           |**Asus4** |

Oh, I really want to know.

           | | |**E**   ‖

C'mon, tell me who are you, you, you, ow, you.

Won't Get Fooled Again

Words and Music by
Peter Townshend

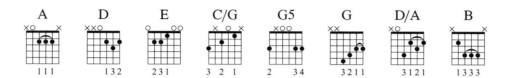

Intro

‖: A | | | :‖

Verse 1

‖ A | D
We'll be fighting in the streets

| A | D
With our children at our feet

| A | D |E |C/G G5
And the morals that they wor - ship will be gone.

| A | D
And the men who spurred us on

| A | D
Sit in judgement of all wrong,

| A | D |E |C/G G5
They de - cide and the shot - gun sings the song.

Chorus 1

```
       ‖D    A      |D           A      |
I'll tip my hat to the new consti - tution,
       D      A      |D       A      |
Take a bow ___ for the new revo - lution.
       D            A     |D            A      |
Smile and grin ___ at the change all a - round,
       G5                       |E          |
Pick up my guitar and play,
       G5               |E
Just like yesterday,
                |G5                    |D    G  |D   G  |D
Then I'll get on my knees and pray,
                |                       ‖
We won't get fooled again.
```

Interlude 1

```
|A          |G5    D |A          |  G5 D  |
        No, no!
|A          |       D |A          |D/A         |
```

Bridge

```
       ‖B                |             |E
I'll move myself and my fam'ly aside,
                         |
If we happen to be left half alive,
       |A                            |
I'll get all my papers and smile __ at the sky,
       |B                            |        ‖
Oh, I know that the hypnotized never lie.
```

Interlude 2

```
|B         | A  E |B         | A  E ‖
```

Guitar Solo

```
|B         | A  E |B         | A  E |
|B         | A  E |B         |        ‖
```

Interlude 3

```
|A         |G5  D |A         |G5   D |
|A         |G5  D |A         |G5   D
 Yeah!
```

56

Verse 2

```
            ‖A                  |        D
There's nothing in the street
              |A              |    G5  D
Looks any different to me.
              |A              |       G5  D      |E            |C/G  G5
And the slogans are re - placed by ___ the by.
              |A             |       D
And the parting on the left
              |A                 |      D
Is now parting on the right,
              |A                            |       D        |E          |C/G  G5
And the beards have all grown long - er o - vernight.
```

Chorus 2

```
              ‖D     A       |D         A        |
I'll tip my hat to the new consti - tution,
D          A        |D          A        |
Take a bow ___ for the new revo - lution.
D            A       |D           A          |
Smile and grin ___ at the change all a - round,
G5                          |E           |
Pick up my guitar and play,
G5                |E
Just like yesterday,
              |G5                  |D          |          ‖
Then I'll get on my knees and pray.
```

Outro

```
|A                  |G5    D  |A                      |G5    D    |
 Yeah!
|A                  |G5    D  |A                      |G5    D   ‖
 Meet the new boss;            same as the old boss.              |
|A                  |        D  |A              |        D   |
|A                  |           |               |           ‖
```

You Better You Bet

Words and Music by
Peter Townshend

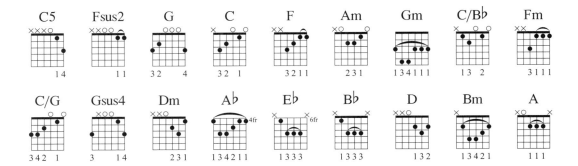

Intro

```
‖: C5        |        :‖

‖: C5     |                        | Fsus2    | G     :‖
   (You better, you better, you bet.      Ooh.)        Play 4 times
```

Verse 1

```
   C                |
   I call you on the telephone,
   | F            G  |        | C
   My voice too rough with cig - arettes.
                          |
   I sometimes feel I should just go home,
      | F            G  |          | C
   But I'm deal - in' with a memory that never forgets.
                          |
   I love to hear ya say my name,
      | F         G  |    | C
   Es - pecially when you say yes.
                          |
   I got your body right now on my mind
         | F                | G              ‖
   But I drank ___ myself blind to the sound of old T. Rex.
```

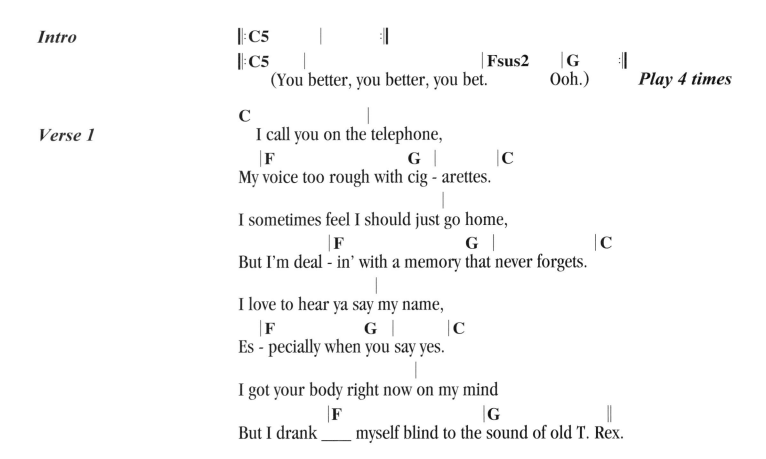

Pre-Chorus 1

Am | |Gm |F |C/B♭ |

Hmm.

|F | |Fm | |

To the sound ___ of old T. Rex.

C/G | |Gsus4 |G ||

Oh,   and *Who's Next*.

Chorus 1

C | |F

When I say I love you, you say, "You better."

|Am   G |C

(You better, you better, you bet.)

| |F

When I say I need you, you say, "You better."

|Am   G |Dm |

(You better, you better, you bet.)

Am |G |

You better bet your life,

|Dm | Am |G | ||

Or love will cut you, (cut you) like a   knife.

Verse 2

C | |F |G |C

I want those fee - ble-minded axes overthrown.

| |F

I'm not into your pass - port picture,

|G |C

I just like your nose.

| |F |G |C

You welcome me with o - pen arms ___ and open legs.

| |F |G ||

I know only fools have needs, but this one never begs.

Pre-Chorus 2

Am | |Gm |F

I don't really mind how much you love me.

|C/B♭ |

Ooh, a little is al - right.

|F | |Fm |

When you say, "Come over and spend the night."

|Gsus4 | | |G ||

Tonight, ___   to - night.

Chorus 2   *Repeat Chorus 1*

Bridge

Ab |Eb
   I lay on the bed ____ with you.
Bb |C |Ab
We could make some book of records.
         |Eb
Your dog keeps lickin' my nose
 |Bb |Dm   Am|G |Dm
And chewing up all those letters saying "You better."
         Am|G | ||
You better bet your life.
||:Am   G Am| G Am |
 (You better love me   all the time, now.
C   G   C | G   C :||
You better shove me back into line, now.)

Guitar Solo

|Am G Am | G Am|C G   C| G C |
|Am G Am | G Am|C G   C| ||

C |

Verse 3

   I showed up late one night
       |F |G |C
With a ne - on light for a visa.
        |
But knowing I'm so ea - ger to fight,
      |F |G |C
Can't make letting me in any eas - ier.
         |
I know I been wearing crazy clothes
  |F |G |C
And I look pretty crappy sometimes,
       |
But my body feels so good
      |F |G ||
And I still ____ sing a razor line ev'ry time.

Am | |Gm |F |C/Bb |

Pre-Chorus 3

      And when it comes ____ to all night living,
           |F | |Fm
I know what I'm giving.
      | |C/G |
I've got it all down to a tee.
     |Gsus4 |G ||
And it's free.

Chorus 3

    C | |F

When I say I love you, you say, "You better."

     |Am   G |C

(You better, you better, you bet.)

                           | |F

When I say I need you, you say, "You better."

     |Am   G |C

(You better, you better, you bet.)

                         | |F

When I say I love you, you say, "You better."

     |Am   G |C

(You better, you better, you bet.)

                         | |F

When I say I need you, you scream, "You better."

     |Am   G |D

(You better, you better, you bet.)

                         | |G

When I say I love you, you say, "You better."

    |Bm   A |D

(You better, you better, you bet.)

                         | |G

When I say I need you, you say, "You better."

    |Bm   A |D

(You better, you better, you bet.)

                         | |G

When I say I love you, you say, "You better."

    |Bm   A |D

(You better, you better, you bet.)

                         | |G

And when I say I need you, you scream, "You better."

    |Bm   A |G |A |G |A |G

(You better, you better, you bet.)

      |A |G |A |G

You ___ better bet your life.

          |A |G |A |G   ‖

Or love will cut you   just like a knife.

STRUM & SING

Lyrics, chord symbols, and guitar chord diagrams for your favorite songs.

GUITAR

ACOUSTIC CLASSICS
00191891..........$12.99

ADELE
00159855..........$12.99

SARA BAREILLES
00102354..........$12.99

THE BEATLES
00172234..........$16.99

BLUES
00159335..........$12.99

ZAC BROWN BAND
02501620..........$12.99

COLBIE CAILLAT
02501725..........$14.99

CAMPFIRE FOLK SONGS
02500686..........$12.99

CHART HITS OF 2014-2015
00142554..........$12.99

CHART HITS OF 2015-2016
00156248..........$12.99

BEST OF KENNY CHESNEY
00142457..........$14.99

CHRISTMAS SONGS
00171332..........$14.99

KELLY CLARKSON
00146384..........$14.99

JOHN DENVER COLLECTION
02500632..........$9.95

EAGLES
00157994..........$12.99

EASY ACOUSTIC SONGS
00125478..........$14.99

50 CHILDREN'S SONGS
02500825..........$9.99

THE 5 CHORD SONGBOOK
02501718..........$12.99

FOLK SONGS
02501482..........$10.99

FOLK/ROCK FAVORITES
02501669..........$10.99

THE 4 CHORD SONGBOOK
02501533..........$12.99

THE 4-CHORD COUNTRY SONGBOOK
00114936..........$14.99

THE GREATEST SHOWMAN
00278383..........$14.99

HAMILTON
00217116..........$14.99

HITS OF THE '70S
02500871..........$9.99

HYMNS
02501125..........$8.99

JACK JOHNSON
02500858..........$16.99

ROBERT JOHNSON
00191890..........$12.99

CAROLE KING
00115243..........$10.99

BEST OF GORDON LIGHTFOOT
00139393..........$14.99

DAVE MATTHEWS BAND
02501078..........$10.95

JOHN MAYER
02501636..........$10.99

INGRID MICHAELSON
02501634..........$10.99

THE MOST REQUESTED SONGS
02501748..........$12.99

JASON MRAZ
02501452..........$14.99

PRAISE & WORSHIP
00152381..........$12.99

ELVIS PRESLEY
00198890..........$12.99

QUEEN
00218578..........$12.99

ROCK AROUND THE CLOCK
00103625..........$12.99

ROCK BALLADS
02500872..........$9.95

ED SHEERAN
00152016..........$14.99

THE 6 CHORD SONGBOOK
02502277..........$10.99

CAT STEVENS
00116827..........$14.99

TAYLOR SWIFT
00159856..........$12.99

THE 3 CHORD SONGBOOK
00211634..........$9.99

TODAY'S HITS
00119301..........$12.99

TOP CHRISTIAN HITS
00156331..........$12.99

TOP HITS OF 2016
00194288..........$12.99

KEITH URBAN
00118558..........$14.99

THE WHO
00103667..........$12.99

NEIL YOUNG – GREATEST HITS
00138270..........$14.99

UKULELE

THE BEATLES
00233899..........$16.99

COLBIE CAILLAT
02501731..........$10.99

JOHN DENVER
02501694..........$10.99

FOLK ROCK FAVORITES FOR UKULELE
00114600..........$9.99

THE 4-CHORD UKULELE SONGBOOK
00114331..........$14.99

JACK JOHNSON
02501702..........$17.99

JOHN MAYER
02501706..........$10.99

INGRID MICHAELSON
02501741..........$12.99

THE MOST REQUESTED SONGS
02501453..........$14.99

JASON MRAZ
02501753..........$14.99

SING-ALONG SONGS
02501710..........$15.99

HAL•LEONARD®

www.halleonard.com
Visit our website to see full song lists.

Prices, content, and availability subject to change without notice.

AUTHENTIC CHORDS • ORIGINAL KEYS • COMPLETE SONGS

The *Strum It* series lets players strum the chords and sing along with their favorite hits. Each song has been selected because it can be played with regular open chords, barre chords, or other moveable chord types. Guitarists can simply play the rhythm, or play and sing along through the entire song. All songs are shown in their original keys complete with chords, strum patterns, melody and lyrics. Wherever possible, the chord voicings from the recorded versions are notated.

THE BEACH BOYS' GREATEST HITS
00699357.............................. $12.95

THE BEATLES FAVORITES
00699249..............................$15.99

VERY BEST OF JOHNNY CASH
00699514..............................$14.99

CELTIC GUITAR SONGBOOK
00699265..............................$12.99

CHRISTMAS SONGS FOR GUITAR
00699247..............................$10.95

CHRISTMAS SONGS WITH 3 CHORDS
00699487..............................$9.99

VERY BEST OF ERIC CLAPTON
00699560..............................$12.95

JIM CROCE – CLASSIC HITS
00699269..............................$10.95

DISNEY FAVORITES
00699171..............................$12.99

MELISSA ETHERIDGE GREATEST HITS
00699518..............................$12.99

FAVORITE SONGS WITH 3 CHORDS
00699112..............................$10.99

FAVORITE SONGS WITH 4 CHORDS
00699270..............................$8.95

FIRESIDE SING-ALONG
00699273..............................$10.99

FOLK FAVORITES
00699517..............................$8.95

THE GUITAR STRUMMERS' ROCK SONGBOOK
00701678..............................$14.99

BEST OF WOODY GUTHRIE
00699496..............................$12.95

JOHN HIATT COLLECTION
00699398..............................$16.99

THE VERY BEST OF BOB MARLEY
00699524..............................$14.99

A MERRY CHRISTMAS SONGBOOK
00699211..............................$9.95

MORE FAVORITE SONGS WITH 3 CHORDS
00699532..............................$9.99

THE VERY BEST OF TOM PETTY
00699336..............................$14.99

ELVIS! GREATEST HITS
00699276..............................$10.95

BEST OF GEORGE STRAIT
00699235..............................$16.99

TAYLOR SWIFT FOR ACOUSTIC GUITAR
00109717..............................$16.99

BEST OF HANK WILLIAMS JR.
00699224..............................$15.99

Prices, contents & availability subject to change without notice.

HAL•LEONARD®

Visit Hal Leonard online at
www.halleonard.com

EASY GUITAR WITH NOTES & TAB

This series features simplified arrangements with notes, tab, chord charts, and strum and pick patterns.

MIXED FOLIOS

00702287 Acoustic	$16.99
00702002 Acoustic Rock Hits for Easy Guitar	$14.99
00702166 All-Time Best Guitar Collection	$19.99
00699665 Beatles Best	$14.99
00702232 Best Acoustic Songs for Easy Guitar	$14.99
00119835 Best Children's Songs	$16.99
00702233 Best Hard Rock Songs	$14.99
00703055 The Big Book of Nursery Rhymes & Children's Songs	$16.99
00322179 The Big Easy Book of Classic Rock Guitar	$24.95
00698978 Big Christmas Collection	$17.99
00702394 Bluegrass Songs for Easy Guitar	$12.99
00703387 Celtic Classics	$14.99
00224808 Chart Hits of 2016-2017	$14.99
00702149 Children's Christian Songbook	$9.99
00702237 Christian Acoustic Favorites	$12.95
00702028 Christmas Classics	$8.99
00101779 Christmas Guitar	$14.99
00702185 Christmas Hits	$9.95
00702141 Classic Rock	$8.95
00702203 CMT's 100 Greatest Country Songs	$27.95
00702283 The Contemporary Christian Collection	$16.99

00702239 Country Classics for Easy Guitar	$19.99
00702282 Country Hits of 2009–2010	$14.99
00702257 Easy Acoustic Guitar Songs	$14.99
00702280 Easy Guitar Tab White Pages	$29.99
00702041 Favorite Hymns for Easy Guitar	$10.99
00140841 4-Chord Hymns for Guitar	$7.99
00702281 4 Chord Rock	$10.99
00126894 Frozen	$14.99
00702286 Glee	$16.99
00699374 Gospel Favorites	$16.99
00122138 The Grammy Awards® Record of the Year 1958-2011	$19.99
00702160 The Great American Country Songbook	$16.99
00702050 Great Classical Themes for Easy Guitar	$8.99
00702116 Greatest Hymns for Guitar	$10.99
00702130 The Groovy Years	$9.95
00702184 Guitar Instrumentals	$9.95
00148030 Halloween Guitar Songs	$14.99
00702273 Irish Songs	$12.99
00702275 Jazz Favorites for Easy Guitar	$15.99
00702274 Jazz Standards for Easy Guitar	$15.99
00702162 Jumbo Easy Guitar Songbook	$19.99
00702258 Legends of Rock	$14.99
00702261 Modern Worship Hits	$14.99

00702189 MTV's 100 Greatest Pop Songs	$24.95
00702272 1950s Rock	$15.99
00702271 1960s Rock	$15.99
00702270 1970s Rock	$15.99
00702269 1980s Rock	$15.99
00702268 1990s Rock	$15.99
00109725 Once	$14.99
00702187 Selections from O Brother Where Art Thou?	$15.99
00702178 100 Songs for Kids	$14.99
00702515 Pirates of the Caribbean	$14.99
00702125 Praise and Worship for Guitar	$10.99
00702285 Southern Rock Hits	$12.99
00121535 30 Easy Celtic Guitar Solos	$14.99
00702220 Today's Country Hits	$9.95
00121900 Today's Women of Pop & Rock	$14.99
00283786 Top Hits of 2018	$14.99
00702294 Top Worship Hits	$15.99
00702255 VH1's 100 Greatest Hard Rock Songs	$27.99
00702175 VH1's 100 Greatest Songs of Rock and Roll	$24.95
00702253 Wicked	$12.99

ARTIST COLLECTIONS

00702267 AC/DC for Easy Guitar	$15.99
00702598 Adele for Easy Guitar	$15.99
00702040 Best of the Allman Brothers	$15.99
00702865 J.S. Bach for Easy Guitar	$14.99
00702169 Best of The Beach Boys	$12.99
00702292 The Beatles — 1	$19.99
00125796 Best of Chuck Berry	$14.99
00702201 The Essential Black Sabbath	$12.95
02501615 Zac Brown Band — The Foundation	$16.99
02501621 Zac Brown Band — You Get What You Give	$16.99
00702043 Best of Johnny Cash	$16.99
00702263 Best of Casting Crowns	$14.99
00702090 Eric Clapton's Best	$10.95
00702086 Eric Clapton — from the Album Unplugged	$10.95
00702202 The Essential Eric Clapton	$14.99
00702250 blink-182 — Greatest Hits	$15.99
00702053 Best of Patsy Cline	$14.99
00702229 The Very Best of Creedence Clearwater Revival	$15.99
00702145 Best of Jim Croce	$15.99
00702278 Crosby, Stills & Nash	$12.99
00702219 David Crowder*Band Collection	$12.95
14042809 Bob Dylan	$14.99
00702276 Fleetwood Mac — Easy Guitar Collection	$14.99
00139462 The Very Best of Grateful Dead	$15.99
00702136 Best of Merle Haggard	$12.99
00702227 Jimi Hendrix — Smash Hits	$14.99
00702288 Best of Hillsong United	$12.99
00702236 Best of Antonio Carlos Jobim	$14.99

00702245 Elton John — Greatest Hits 1970–2002	$14.99
00129855 Jack Johnson	$15.99
00702204 Robert Johnson	$10.99
00702234 Selections from Toby Keith — 35 Biggest Hits	$12.95
00702003 Kiss	$10.99
00110578 Best of Kutless	$12.99
00702216 Lynyrd Skynyrd	$15.99
00702182 The Essential Bob Marley	$14.94
00146081 Maroon 5	$14.99
00121925 Bruno Mars – Unorthodox Jukebox	$12.99
00702248 Paul McCartney — All the Best	$14.99
00702129 Songs of Sarah McLachlan	$12.95
00125484 The Best of MercyMe	$12.99
02501316 Metallica — Death Magnetic	$19.99
00702209 Steve Miller Band — Young Hearts (Greatest Hits)	$12.95
00124167 Jason Mraz	$15.99
00702096 Best of Nirvana	$15.99
00702211 The Offspring — Greatest Hits	$12.95
00138026 One Direction	$14.99
00702030 Best of Roy Orbison	$14.99
00702144 Best of Ozzy Osbourne	$14.99
00702279 Tom Petty	$12.99
00102911 Pink Floyd	$16.99
00702139 Elvis Country Favorites	$14.99
00702293 The Very Best of Prince	$15.99
00699415 Best of Queen for Guitar	$14.99
00109279 Best of R.E.M.	$14.99
00702208 Red Hot Chili Peppers — Greatest Hits	$14.99

00198960 The Rolling Stones	$16.99
00174793 The Very Best of Santana	$14.99
00702196 Best of Bob Seger	$12.95
00146046 Ed Sheeran	$14.99
00702252 Frank Sinatra — Nothing But the Best	$12.99
00702010 Best of Rod Stewart	$16.99
00702049 Best of George Strait	$14.99
00702259 Taylor Swift for Easy Guitar	$15.99
00702260 Taylor Swift — Fearless	$14.99
00139727 Taylor Swift — 1989	$17.99
00115960 Taylor Swift — Red	$16.99
00253667 Taylor Swift — Reputation	$17.99
00702290 Taylor Swift — Speak Now	$15.99
00702226 Chris Tomlin — See the Morning	$12.95
00148643 Train	$14.99
00702427 U2 — 18 Singles	$16.99
00102711 Van Halen	$16.99
00702108 Best of Stevie Ray Vaughan	$16.99
00702123 Best of Hank Williams	$14.99
00702111 Stevie Wonder — Guitar Collection	$9.95
00702228 Neil Young — Greatest Hits	$15.99
00119133 Neil Young — Harvest	$14.99
00702188 Essential ZZ Top	$10.95

Prices, contents and availability subject to change without notice.

HAL•LEONARD®

Visit Hal Leonard online at
www.halleonard.com

0818